ASH WEDNESDAY

Yet even now, says the Lo
all your heart, wit
and with mournin
and not your clothi
—JOEL 2:12–18

On the first day of Lent God pleads with us to return home. God patiently watches over us as we wander and lose our way, waiting with us through our confusion. God always believes in us and our goodness—which is a good thing because, too often, we lose faith in our own goodness.

There is a story about a Sunday school teacher who was trying to teach her fifth-grade class about good and evil. As she was finishing her lesson, she told the class that God saw all the good people as red and all the bad people as white. Then she asked the class this question, "If all the good people are red and all the bad people are white, what color are you?" The response was somewhat predictable. All the good children quickly got recognized and announced to the class that they were red. All the children who thought of themselves as bad remained quiet. That left Sally wildly waving her hand in a desperate attempt to be recognized by the teacher. Based on past experience, the teacher was trying to ignore Sally but she would not be denied. Finally the teacher capitulated and said, "OK, Sally, if all the good people are red and all the bad people are white, what color would you be?" Sally blurted out, "Streaky!"

What a great answer; what total honesty! Sally was not speaking just for herself, she was speaking for all of us. We are at best streaky. Sometimes we are good and sometimes we are bad. Too often we learn to live with our checkerboard existence, a life that is filled with squares of goodness and squares of evil. Lent is, or can be, a trumpet call from God begging us not to settle for mediocrity. God made us in his image and wants us to be good. Lent is a gift from God, an opportunity to examine our streaky behavior and root out what is evil.

PRAYER ***Lord of time and history, we have abused your gifts. Help us root out all that prevents us from being your sons and daughters.***

THURSDAY AFTER ASH WEDNESDAY

Moses said to the people: "Today I have set before you life and prosperity, death and doom."
—DEUTERONOMY 30:15–20

Life is all about choices. In today's first reading Moses reminds us that God puts before us choices that will lead to life and prosperity, and choices that will lead to death. In the gospel, Jesus reminds us that if we are to follow him we must be willing to take up our cross each and every day. What is that cross? The cross is making the right choice.

Whenever I think of choices and the values that propel our choices, I think of yard sales (tag sales, garage sales, whatever they are called in your neck of the woods). Yard sales are a living memorial to the fact that we make wrong choices. I have never actually been to a yard sale, although I have from time to time slowed down as I have driven by one. Yard sales are all about bad choices. We buy things that we think are going to make us happy. Some things actually do bring a modicum of happiness; others never make it out of the box. When we have accumulated a sufficient number of no longer useful items, we put them out on the front lawn and sell them. Why do we sell them? So we can get more money to buy more things that will not satisfy. It is a vicious circle. What we ought to do is put all the stuff in the front yard with a sign that says, "We no longer need these things, take what you want."

Lent is an opportunity to have a yard sale of the mind and heart. It is an invitation to examine the attitudes, values, hopes, and dreams that energize our lives. We need to clean out the attic of our minds where all our false hopes and shallow values corrupt our choices. Lent will work if, and only if, we are willing to realize we are wasting our time if we continue to pile up possessions but lose ourselves in the process.

PRAYER ***O God, giver of all good gifts, help us identify anything that clutters up our lives, and help us remove anything that prevents us from being better believers.***

FRIDAY AFTER ASH WEDNESDAY

When Jesus had crossed over into the territory of the Gerasenes, John's disciples came to him with the objection, "Why is it that while we and the Pharisees fast, your disciples do not?"
—MATTHEW 9:14–15

The disciples of the Pharisees and John the Baptist are worried about why Jesus' disciples are not fasting. Why were the disciples of the Pharisees worried about the fasting of others? Because their own fasting was a failure. Fasting should fine-tune our senses so we can more fully appreciate the goodness in the world, not help us be more critical.

Unfortunately most of us have bought the fallacy that life is supposed to be happy, not require much work, and certainly not call for sacrifice. There should be a pill for every problem and a quick fix for every failure. Madison Avenue sells us this lie and we gladly buy it. Fact of the matter is, all positive life experiences require discipline and sacrifice. Marriage, family, relationships, success, prayer—each of these realities has the power to bring us great personal happiness. Is there a happy marriage that does not require hard work and personal sacrifice? Is there a strong family unit that magically happens?

Prayer that has the power to transform us requires immense discipline and scavenged time. We need to set aside prayer time because the time will not just appear magically in the midst of our schedules. Unless we pray every day, we will not grow spiritually. And we must pray in creative ways. Most of us have a series of favorite prayers that we say every day. Most of us manage to squeeze in morning or evening prayers but how long do they last? A few minutes at best. One thing is certain, we will never grow in our appreciation of God's love in a few, memorized prayers that are said half-awake or half-asleep. Some people are morning people, others are evening people. We know which one we are. Now the challenge is to set aside some time during our best period of the day and give it to God in prayer.

PRAYER ***You are the God we choose to serve. May our sacrifices and our fasting lead us closer to you.***

SATURDAY AFTER ASH WEDNESDAY

After this he went out and saw a tax collector named Levi sitting at the tax booth; and he said to him, "Follow me." And he got up, left everything, and followed him.

—LUKE 5:27–32

I often wonder how many times Jesus called Levi before he finally answered. In today's gospel, it sounds as if Jesus went up to Levi, called him, and Levi followed: end of story. If that is what happened, then today's gospel has nothing to teach us because it is foreign to our faith journey.

In Levi's life and in ours, it is more a question of God wearing us down than of us joyfully responding. God calls us over and over again. We hear; we feign deafness. We are sure God must have made a mistake. How could God possibly want me when there are so many better qualified people in the world? Levi must have asked this same question. He was a tax collector, and so he was an outcast. People avoided him because of his profession. But Jesus called him, he answered, and we have this gospel that has led untold numbers of people to meet Jesus.

The same is true for us. God calls us over and over again. We are sure he has made a mistake. We are weak; we are fickle. We are too selfish, quick tempered, and obstinate. Surely God can find better people elsewhere. Of course he can and he does, but that does not let us off the hook. Just as there were people only Levi could bring to the Lord, so there are people only we can bring to God. The more broken and fragile we are, the more God needs us. Since God uses the weak to confront the strong, we are just the people he is looking for to bring home the message that God works through us. Just as Michelangelo looked at a flawed piece of marble and saw David, so God looks at us with all our flaws and sees believers.

So perhaps today's "Follow me" will be the one that finally wears us down. If not, perhaps tomorrow will be the day.

PRAYER ***God of the call, help us remove anything that prevents us from hearing you call us to be your followers.***

FIRST SUNDAY OF LENT

Jesus, full of the Holy Spirit, returned from the Jordan and was led by the Spirit into the wilderness, where for forty days he was tempted by the devil.
—LUKE 4:1–13

Temptation is part of every life. Unfortunately, most of us are experts in giving in to temptation and rationalizing our behavior. Lent is a gift from God, a gift which invites us to examine our temptations and believe, once again, that with God's help we do not have to be the victims of our temptations.

Here is a perfect lenten story. A young boy walks into a drugstore and asks the owner if he can use the phone. He is given permission and the pharmacist overhears this conversation: "Hello, Dr. Brown, do you want to hire a boy to cut your lawn and run errands for you? Oh, you already have a boy doing that and you are completely satisfied with his efforts. OK, good-bye." The pharmacist says to the boy, "Son, if you are looking for a job, I could use a boy like you." The boy says, "I already have a job. I work for Dr. Brown. I was just checking up on myself!" That is what Lent is all about. Lent is a time to check up on ourselves.

Our lives get cluttered with junk which prevents us from dedicating ourselves to what is good. We get lost in our busyness. We surround ourselves with noise and distractions. The ubiquitous cell phone has managed to violate every space in our lives. Our memories become so clogged with past offenses that we cannot see the forest for the trees. The pain of a divorce blurs everything we do. The random act of an insensitive priest pollutes all of our churchgoing. Our dysfunctional family makes us fearful of all intimate relationships.

We need to check up on ourselves, to take an honest look at who we are and see if we like who we have become. Lent is the time to clear the attic of our memories of every excuse we use to fail.

PRAYER ***Jesus, you spent forty days and forty nights in the desert wrestling with the devil. Be with us during this lenten season and help us believe once again that we can triumph over our temptations.***

MONDAY OF THE FIRST WEEK

The Lord spoke to Moses, saying: "Speak to all the congregation of the people of Israel and say to them: You shall be holy, for I the Lord your God am holy. You shall not steal; you shall not deal falsely; and you shall not lie to one another."

—LEVITICUS 19:1–2, 11–18

The chosen people of the original covenant developed an intricate set of rules that organized every aspect of life. They could walk only so far on the Sabbath. They could eat only certain foods, their young boys had to be circumcised. There were rules for divorce, rules for tithing, rules for worship, rules for what you were to do if your brother died and left a wife and no children. Rules, rules, rules!

We, the chosen people of the new covenant, are as rule-bound, if not more so, than our spiritual ancestors. We were not content with the commandments of God—we created the commandments of the Church. We have rules that come with the penalty of mortal sin and those that are judged to be but venial sins. Sometimes we hide behind our rules and sometimes we just run away from them, but there are always rules, rules, and more rules.

One day two monks, one older and one younger, were out for a walk. They came upon a river swollen by recent rains. As they tried to figure out a way to cross the river, they caught sight of a young woman who was also trying to find a way across. The young monk walked over to the woman, picked her up, and carried her to the other side. The older monk stormed across the river and caught up with the young monk. They continued their journey in silence, but after a time the older monk said, "You should not have done that. You know we are forbidden to have contact with women!" The young monk looked kindly upon the older monk and said, "I put the woman down on the other side of the river, and you are still carrying her."

PRAYER ***God of love, help us appreciate more fully that the only law that should rule our lives is the law of love.***

TUESDAY OF THE FIRST WEEK

When you are praying, do not heap up empty phrases as the Gentiles do; for they think that they will be heard because of their many words.

—MATTHEW 6:7–15

The town of Bastongne in Belgium has a museum called the "Nuts Museum," which is dedicated to the Battle of the Bulge. As the story goes, the Germans were winning their battle with the American soldiers. The commander of the German troops sent word to the commander of the American troops, General Anthony C. McAuliffe, and asked if he was ready to surrender. General McAuliffe gave a one-word answer, "Nuts!" The Germans were not familiar enough with American slang to know what he meant. They were not sure if McAuliffe was trying to speak Russian and say, "Nyet." They were confused by one word. While they tried to figure out what the General meant, McAuliffe was able to reorganize his troops and, as we know from history, snatch victory from the jaws of defeat. One word changed the course of history.

This past Christmas, my brother Mike used his computer to create a very personal calendar. On the calendar he put a picture of my father, who had died a year earlier. Next to the picture he printed a series of my father's favorite quotes: "Better to have it and not need it than to need it and not have it." "Many a young man has been deprived of working hard at precisely those things that made a man of his father." "A pleasure twice deferred is a pleasure thrice enjoyed." "Young man, your dream of sweet young life is over." Mike gave me a copy of that calendar, and it has given me great joy. My father is dead but his words live on, as does his wisdom.

This Lent, spend some time calling to mind the quotes of significant people who have preceded us through the gates of death. Let their words speak to us with new and deeper meaning. Then we can go back to the Scriptures and let the words of Jesus speak to us once again with a richness and force we may have lost in the busyness of our lives.

PRAYER ***Almighty God, you sent your Word to heal and redeem us. Help us embrace your Word and transform our lives.***

WEDNESDAY OF THE FIRST WEEK

When the crowds were increasing, he began to say, "This generation is an evil generation; it asks for a sign, but no sign will be given to it except the sign of Jonah."

—LUKE 11:29–32

One of the greatest signs of faith that I have been privileged to experience is the love and hope shown by family members when someone they love slips into an irreversible coma. Inspired by stories of previous coma victims who come to after many months, even years, of unconsciousness, these people sit by the hour at their loved one's bedside. They carry on conversations, they tell stories, they hold hands and tenderly caress the silent patient. They know, or better, they believe that the patient can hear everything they say.

But we all have our limits. As the coma seems endless, hope begins to diminish. Daily visits become every-other-day visits, and visits become shorter and shorter. Their vigil grows silent, the only words being prayers and expressions of love as the patient sinks deeper and deeper into an unresponsive world.

God showers us with signs of both his presence and his will. Yet we ignore what is and ask for what we already have in abundance. We want signs but God knows we have grown too adept at ignoring the signs he has already sent. We hear the squeak of the fan belt but we do not act until the battery is dead. Our body gives us all kinds of signs that something is wrong but we don't go to the doctor until it is almost too late. Our spouse grows more and more distant yet we are surprised when confronted with our callousness. Our prayer becomes less and less frequent, attendance at Mass perfunctory and irregular, yet we complain about the absence of God in our lives.

Why should God waste his time sending us new signs when we have ignored the old ones?

PRAYER ***Throughout our lives you are the God who speaks to us through signs and wonders. We do not ask that you send more signs but that you help us interpret the signs that already enrich our lives.***

THURSDAY OF THE FIRST WEEK

Ask, and it will be given you; search, and you will find; knock, and the door will be opened for you.
—MATTHEW 7:7–12

Why is good advice so hard to follow? Prayer should be easy but we make it difficult. When it comes to prayer, simple is best. Our own words will always have more power than borrowed words; nevertheless, we feel more comfortable with the prayers of others. We all know that prayer is a conversation with God; we know that God loves us, and we know that when we speak with a lover words flow from our heart, not our mind. We know all this, yet we do not trust it when it comes to our conversations with God.

All of us have been in situations where we wanted to impress someone. When we have to ask someone for a big favor, we practice what we are going to say. Sometimes we even try to memorize what we are going to say. The result is that we make a mess of our presentation. There is no spontaneity. There is no warmth. There is no vulnerability. If we are lucky, we get to throw away the script and just be ourselves.

A number of years ago, I went to my parents to ask for financial help. I arrived home, cleared the kitchen table, spread out some blueprints, and made my presentation, which took about twenty minutes. My father was a man of few words. He had listened attentively to my presentation. When I was finished he said, "You just wasted twenty minutes of my time." My heart sank as my dream went up in smoke. Then my father smiled and said, "Of course we will loan you the money—why did you feel you had to make a presentation to us as though we were strangers?"

When I later reflected on my conversation with my parents, I concluded that I had not had a conversation with them. I gave them a presentation when a conversation was all that was needed. Too often I do the same with God; I suspect that I am not alone in doing so.

PRAYER ***For perhaps the first time, we come before you, God, without the prayers of others. Help us to trust that your love will fill the empty words we often present to you.***

FRIDAY OF THE FIRST WEEK

So when you are offering your gift at the altar, if you remember that your brother or sister has something against you, leave your gift there before the altar and go; first be reconciled to your brother or sister, and then come and offer your gift.

—MATTHEW 5:20–26

There is something tremendously unfair about today's Scripture passage. If my sister or brother has something against me, that is their problem not mine. We have enough trouble dealing with what we have against brother and sister without taking on their problems. Besides, our sisters and brothers are too often unreasonable. They are too demanding, they expect too much from us. It is unhealthy to live according to the expectations of others.

Now that we have that straightened out, we can get on with our lives. We can determine who should be offended, who should be insulted, and who should feel rejected. When we put it that way, it sounds a bit harsh, doesn't it? Perhaps we need to revisit the issue of how we determine who is on the outs with us. Perhaps Jesus was on to something when he gave what at first sounded like a twisted way of measuring offense. If someone is offended but we did not mean to offend them, they are still offended and some action is needed. Even an unintended offense needs an apology.

There is no doubt that the challenge in today's gospel is going to strike some of us as scrupulous at worst and pre-scrupulous at best. Nevertheless, if we would all live out the challenge, is there any doubt that our world would be a more loving and more caring place? If we continue to decide who has the right to be insulted or offended, there are going to be a lot of hurt people in the world—and indeed, there already are. Jesus offers us a way to remove the hurt that too often follows in our wake, the way of peace and reconciliation.

PRAYER ***You are the God of forgiveness. You have shown us how to live but we have resisted you. Help us this day to be at peace with all of our sisters and brothers.***

SATURDAY OF THE FIRST WEEK

But I say to you, love your enemies and pray for those who persecute you so that you may be children of your father in heaven; for he makes his sun rise on the evil and on the good, and sends rain on the righteous and on the unrighteous.

—MATTHEW 5:43–48

At first glance, the challenge of today's gospel might seem to be more than we can do. Fortunately, Jesus understands our human nature all too well. As a result, he does not tell us to be nice to our enemies; he tells us to pray for our enemies. Jesus' command shows conclusively that he did indeed take on our human nature. As a result he asks for prayers before deeds.

Unfortunately, all of us have enemies. We have people we avoid, people with whom we do not speak. Whatever the place or status of our enemies, now is the time to begin praying for them. While we are at it, we should say a prayer for ourselves as well. Praying for enemies offers us plenty of latitude. We can pray that they change. We can pray that they give up their selfish, obnoxious ways. We can pray that they will grow on us. Of course, we can offer the same prayers for ourselves.

Prayer will not solve every problem but it will point us in the right direction. Here is a delightful story that highlights this power of prayer. Mark and his younger sister Susie were having one of their frequent sibling spats. When Susie was saying her prayers before going to bed, her Mom was listening intently to see if Susie would mention her brother. She did not. Mom, acting in the place of Jesus, said to Susie, "What about your brother?" Susie, knowing that there was no escape, got back down on her knees and said, "And God, please remember my ex-brother, Mark." Her prayer is a long way from reconciliation but at least it is a start. Why not pick an enemy and offer a prayer, however feeble. It could be the first small step in the right direction.

PRAYER ***Throughout history the people your love has called into existence have turned away from your love. Help us return to you by loving and praying for those we consider enemies.***

SECOND SUNDAY OF LENT

Now about eight days after these sayings Jesus took with him Peter and John and James, and went up on the mountain to pray. And while he was praying, the appearance of his face changed and his clothes became dazzling white.

—LUKE 9:28–36

The Transfiguration represents a breakthrough moment in the lives of Peter, James, and John. On that mountain, they saw and experienced more in Jesus than had previously been the case. The experience came upon them by surprise, and they did not know what to do. All they knew was that they saw more in Jesus and, in so doing, realized that they had to see more in themselves.

Author Stephen Covey, in his book *Seven Habits of Highly Effective People*, shares a transfiguration experience with his readers. He tells of how he was riding the subway one Sunday morning when a man and his children got on. Soon all was in chaos. The children were screaming and running all about. One of them even grabbed a newspaper out of one man's hands. Through it all, the father sat passively unaware of the havoc being wrought by his children. Finally, in exasperation, Mr. Covey went over to the man and said, "Sir, your children are really disturbing a lot of people. I wonder if you couldn't control them a bit more?" The man snapped out of his trance and said, "Oh, you're right. I guess I should do something about it. We just came from the hospital where their mother died about an hour ago. I don't know what to think, and I guess they don't know how to handle it either." Suddenly Covey saw more in the man, more in the children, and more in the situation. Nothing had changed in the subway car, but now there was understanding and everything was different.

Perhaps we all need to take another look at the things that upset us and see what we might be missing.

PRAYER ***We need your help, God, if we are to see more in others and more in ourselves. Please, give faith to our seeing that we might more fully celebrate the many gifts that already enrich our lives.***

MONDAY OF THE SECOND WEEK

Do not judge and you will not be judged; do not condemn and you will not be condemned. Forgive and you will be forgiven; give and it will be given to you.

—LUKE 6:36–38

Those who know me would probably suggest that in honesty I should just skip a reflection on today's reading. They would be correct because I do judge people. I don't condemn them but I do judge them. Nevertheless, I am fairly good at one of today's commands. I am fairly good at giving to others but all too often my judging others hinders them from seeing my generosity. I do judge but I am not happy with that part of my life and I am working hard to change. So maybe, just maybe, I can offer a reflection on today's reading.

For me, and I suspect I am not alone, the problem with my judging is that too often I am wrong. I judge people without all of the information. I can be very much like Stephen Covey in yesterday's reflection. In truth, aren't we all? The American Indians offer us the wisdom, "Never criticize a man until you have walked a mile in his moccasins." The theory is that once we have crawled inside another person's skin and lived their life, we will be much more understanding of their behavior. Perhaps we can understand their behavior as well as we understand our own. If this happens, then perhaps we can learn to cut others as much slack as we cut ourselves.

One thing is certain, Jesus practiced what he preached. Jesus did not look on others the way most people did. Jesus did not look on sinners and condemn them to remain sinners. He looked on sinners and saw people who could turn their lives around. Rather than focus on bad people, Jesus chose to focus on bad choices made by good people. I remember well the wisdom of the nuns who taught me in grammar school. They used to admonish us to "Hate the sin but love the sinner." Even though I remember their wisdom, I too seldom act upon it.

PRAYER ***It takes so little effort to see the faults and failings of others. And so we humbly ask you to give us the strength to work harder at seeing the goodness in others.***

TUESDAY OF THE SECOND WEEK

The greatest among you will be your servant. All who exalt themselves will be humbled, and all who humble themselves will be exalted.

—MATTHEW 23:1–12

Servanthood is the call of the Christian! We are called to serve the needs of others, called to put others before ourselves. For me the greatest example of being a servant is being a parent. Whenever I see new parents arriving at church, I always say to them, "I bet you have newfound love and respect for your parents." The usual response is non-verbal. They smile and gently nod their heads up and down.

Parents give so freely of their time and energy to children. I know parents who do not get any time for themselves when their children are young. They tell me how wonderful it feels when they can get a baby-sitter and just go out and have dinner by themselves. They savor the moment because it happens so infrequently. Parents humble themselves for their children, and they wait a long time to feel exalted. But you can see the exaltation in the look of joy on parents' faces as they celebrate a daughter or son's wedding. They share in the pride when an adult child is honored with a reward or a big promotion. They revel with delight when they visit with the grandchildren. These moments of exaltation do not come easily; these moments cannot come without the sacrifices demanded. They are purchased with lost sleep, changing diapers, holding a sick child, attending school plays, worried pacing until the car pulls into the driveway, countless teacher meetings, arguments over bedtime, and mistakes lovingly forgiven.

Christianity demands that parents extend their parenting and that those who are not parents adopt the lost and needy to serve their needs. Many times when people call me "Father," I hear it as a gentle reminder to meet their needs as would a loving parent.

PRAYER ***God, whom we dare to call Father, help us deepen our appreciation for our parents and pass on their unconditional love to everyone we meet.***

WEDNESDAY OF THE SECOND WEEK

But Jesus answered, "You do not know what you are asking. Are you able to drink the cup that I am about to drink?" They said to him, "We are able." He said to them, "You will indeed drink my cup, but to sit at my right and my left, this is not mine to grant, but it is for those for whom it has been prepared by my Father."

—MATTHEW 20:17–28

Today's gospel reminds us of the danger of comparisons. James and John and their mother are worried about places of honor in the kingdom of God's love. But the honor of being seated to someone's right or left has meaning only here on earth. We are accustomed to paying more for the better seats; the box seats are more expensive than the bleachers. We have been conditioned to believe that the important people get the best seats. Because of this we fight for the good seats. We forget that the biggest scoundrel in the world can have the best seats in the house, while a truly wonderful person is hidden away in the back rows.

I remember hearing a story about Mother Teresa when she won the Nobel Peace Prize. They sent her a first-class ticket to fly to Sweden to accept her prize. Mother Teresa, whose whole life was dedicated to seeing goodness in people whom society had discarded, accepted the ticket without objection but she never sat in the first-class section. Instead, she exchanged her first-class ticket for a coach ticket and used the money saved to support one of her missionary centers. She did not let herself make comparisons. She knew that despite all the luxury, everyone lands at the same time. She drank from the cup of ordinariness and taught the world a valuable lesson.

In the kingdom of God's love there are no distinctions. We are all loved totally by God. Perhaps we should prepare for the equality of the world to come by making this world a better place for all people.

PRAYER ***Inspired by the example of all your holy men and women, may we learn how to drink from the cup of ordinariness so we can share our surplus with the needy.***

THURSDAY OF THE SECOND WEEK

Abraham said, "Between you and us a great chasm has been fixed, so that those who might want to pass from here to you cannot do so, and no one can cross from there to us."

—LUKE 16:19–31

I have always been fascinated by the "great chasm" between the flames of Hades and the bosom of Abraham, which is heaven. The chasm shows that God truly understands our human nature. Anyone evil enough to end up in the flames would certainly be devious enough to sneak into heaven. After all, they had spent their whole life taking what did not belong to them, while anyone good enough to be in heaven would certainly want to ease the misery of those suffering in the flames. So if heaven and hell are to remain separate, there has to be a "great chasm."

A woman died without ever doing anything good and she was sent to hell as punishment for her wayward life. Her guardian angel was desperate to find something she had done that might lead to her salvation, so he went to God and said, "I know this woman has not lived a good life, but she once took an onion from her garden and gave it to a beggar." God was moved by this glimmer of goodness and gave an onion to the guardian angel to lower into hell so that the old woman could grab on and be lifted out. The angel was thrilled at this last hope for salvation. Gleefully he lowered the onion into hell. The woman grabbed on and was being lifted out of hell. When her fellow sufferers saw that she was being saved, they all grabbed on to her that they too might be saved. The old woman, fearing that she might be pulled back into hell, began to kick and scream for the others to let go. As a result, the onion broke and she sank back into hell for all eternity.

When we think only of ourselves there is no hope of salvation. We need to think of others while we are still alive lest we find ourselves forever in that place of torment.

PRAYER ***We will not change once we are dead. May the love of our God teach us how to be more loving this day and every day.***

FRIDAY OF THE SECOND WEEK

When the tenants saw the son, they said, "This is the heir, come, let us kill him and get his inheritance." So they seized him, threw him out of the vineyard and killed him. Now when the owner of the vineyard comes, what will he do to those tenants?

—MATTHEW 21:33–43, 45–46

Greed is the most insidious of the vices. It can turn even the eyes and hearts of good people to the possessions of others. Greed fuels the desire to have more and more. Greed whets an appetite that can never be satiated and drives us to all sorts of foolish behavior.

In the movie *Zorba the Greek,* there is a chilling scene where an old woman who has been cut off from the other members of the island is near death. The women of the island gather in her home, not to tend to her in her dying but to pounce on her possessions once she is dead. In their greed they fail to wait for her death. Instead they strip her house of all her possessions, even her bed, before the woman is dead. Watching that scene always fills me with horror. How could those people have become so depraved?

We are much more subtle about our greed than the women in that movie. We would never desecrate the home of a dying woman with our greed. We wait until after the death and fight over the will. We have all seen families split over a ring, a car, or the family china. Perhaps we have experienced our own families being divided over such issues.

If we take a pane of glass and hold it up, we can see right through it. If we coat one side of the glass with silver, we create a mirror. When we hold up the mirror, we can only see ourselves. Today's gospel invites us to search our lives and discover where greed has created mirrors; wherever it is, we need to peel away the silver so we can see our sisters and our brothers clearly once again.

PRAYER ***God of all creation, you have showered us with the beauty of creation. May we imitate your generosity by sharing your gifts more fully with all your daughters and sons.***

SATURDAY OF THE SECOND WEEK

I will get up and go to my father and I will say to him, "Father, I have sinned against heaven and before you; I am no longer worthy to be called your son; treat me like one of your hired hands." So he set off and went to his father. But while he was still far off, his father saw him and was filled with compassion; he ran and put his arms around him and kissed him.

—LUKE 15:1–3, 11–32

Jesus never gave titles to his parables; he just told them. It was some pious monk or editor of the Bible many years later who came up with the titles. God would never have titled the parable "The Prodigal Son." We do so because we are more comfortable with our failings than we are with God's love. Focusing on our prodigal nature gives us a feeling of control; focusing on God's love makes us vulnerable.

The most powerful image in the story is where the father sees his lost son still a long way off, making his slow but steady return. The father runs out to meet him and shrinks the distance that separates the two of them. The power of the father's love sweeps aside all obstacles to reunion. The wayward son tries to keep some of the power by reciting his memorized confession, "Father, I do not deserve to be called your son." The father silences him with a hug, a hug which reminds the son that he may not deserve to be called son, but that the father has bestowed sonship on him. He can run away again or he can continue his return, but the father will always call him son.

During Lent, we attempt to root sin out of our lives. We do penance to improve the quality of our lives and the faithfulness of our choices. These behaviors are not bad unless they delude us into thinking that we can earn God's loving forgiveness. But in his total and complete love for us, God gives forgiveness unconditionally; it is not something we must earn. Lent should be a time when we accept the fact of God's love and let that love change our lives.

PRAYER ***We have all wandered from the path of truth and honesty. May today be the day that we turn away from our wandering and set out on the path that will lead us back to God.***

THIRD SUNDAY OF LENT

"For three years, I have come looking for fruit on this fig tree and still I find none. Cut it down! Why should it be wasting the soil?" He replied, "Sir, let it alone for one more year, until I dig around it and put manure on it. If it bears fruit next year, well and good; but if not, you can cut it down."

—LUKE 13:1–9

Fortunately for us, our God is the God of second chances. Second, third, and even fourth chances. Our God never gives up on us. No matter how many times we fail, God always believes that next time we will get it right.

Today's first reading is about Moses, the Moses who was privileged to bring the law to the chosen people; the same Moses who murdered an Egyptian. Moses got a second chance. The second reading is from Paul's second letter to the Corinthians. Paul organized and supervised the martyrdom of Stephen. But Paul, the persecutor, got a second chance and became the Apostle to the Gentiles. The gospel is about a barren fig tree that got a second chance to bear fruit. The Bible is full of people who got a second chance. Peter betrayed Jesus and got a second chance which led to his being the leader of the early church. Zacchaeus, the tax collector, got a second chance and hosted Jesus in his home. Mary Magdalene forgot her dignity but got her second chance. The woman at the well had gone through five husbands and was living with a man. She got seven chances.

The most important message of Christianity is that no matter how many times we have failed, no matter how many times we have sinned, we can never exhaust God's love. God blesses us with his love every day. We are bathed in love, we are nurtured in love, we are immersed in love because our God knows that his love is stronger than our resistance. God is committed to loving us into goodness. No matter what we have done wrong, no matter how many times we have failed, our God will not give up on us.

PRAYER ***Thank you, God, for your unfailing love. Help us see more clearly the goodness you see in us and in all your people.***

MONDAY OF THE THIRD WEEK

And he said, "Truly, I tell you, no prophet is accepted in the prophet's home town."

—LUKE 4:24–30

Jesus returns home. His popularity is well-known throughout the region. The friends he grew up with, the families who were his neighbors flock to the synagogue to hear him. They knew he lacked formal training; indeed, some may have even thought he was uppity, trying to rise above his humble origins. Nevertheless, they wanted to hear him because somehow he had the gift to reach people. He told stories and parables and helped people feel good about themselves.

They gathered in the synagogue and to their amazement, instead of making them feel good about themselves, his words set loose the demon of guilt in their minds. He reminded his audience of friends and neighbors that they had not always trusted God. Naaman the Syrian (a foreigner) had trusted God; the widow of Zarephath near Sidon had trusted God. And God had acted in their lives. He fed the widow and he cured Naaman. Jesus' message was clear—his friends and neighbors had difficulties in their lives because they had not trusted God. No one wants to hear that message. No one wants to be held accountable for the darkness in his life. Not then; not now. The message of Jesus stung them, and it will sting us if we listen with our hearts.

There is a great story about an ocean liner that was caught in stormy weather. The boat was thrown about in the waves for several days. Most of the passengers remained in their cabins. After three days of stormy weather one brave soul ventured out of his cabin. He was pulling himself along the passageway, when he turned a corner and to his wonderment there was a young girl playing jacks. The passenger watched the girl in amazement for several minutes and then said, "Little girl aren't you afraid?" The girl looked up at him and said, "No! My daddy is the captain!" That is the trust God wants from us.

PRAYER ***Dear God, please enlighten our minds that we may never grow rigid in our opinions of others. Help us see the potential in the people around us.***

TUESDAY OF THE THIRD WEEK

For this reason the kingdom of heaven may be compared to a king who wished to settle accounts with his slaves.

—MATTHEW 18:21–35

At first glance the parable of the ungrateful servant is about forgiveness. Yet a deeper reading clearly indicates that the parable is about the love that leads to forgiveness. The king loves the official who owes him money. Because of this love he forgives his debt. The official does not love his fellow servant so he is unable to forgive his debt. For the parable to work, the king shouldn't call the official ungrateful, the king should call him unloving. The official gets all caught up in an "I owe him, you owe me" trap. He is mired in a concept of forgiveness that is more accounting than loving.

Forgiveness is not an easy virtue. Even the concept of "I will be forgiven as I forgive" fails to move our hearts. Forgiveness is difficult because we insist on turning it into accounting. We add up the offenses; we try to blot them out. We wrestle with the conflict between forgiving and forgetting. We pray and ask God to help us be more forgiving but in so doing we miss the boat. Our problem is not with forgiveness; our problem is with loving. Our parents never have trouble forgiving us. The same is true with our friends. Our friends overlook our shortcomings and failures all the time, just as we overlook theirs. Why? Because they truly love us. Forgiveness flows from love. Forgiveness without love is impossible. With love forgiveness flows naturally.

Take a minute to call to mind a person we have failed to forgive. Do not focus on their past offense; focus on why we will not love that person. Once we choose to love them, forgiveness is a moot point because true forgiveness flows from true love.

PRAYER ***You are the God of loving forgiveness. May we allow ourselves to experience your healing love in a way that compels us to heal all the broken relationships in our lives.***

WEDNESDAY OF THE THIRD WEEK

Do not think that I have come to abolish the law or the prophets; I have come not to abolish but to fulfill.
—MATTHEW 5:17–19

Fulfilling the prophets was easier than fulfilling the law. The people were waiting for the prophets to be fulfilled; the law was another case entirely. The law was meant to guide and lead, to organize and facilitate; it was meant to lead people to God. Instead it had become a tool to remind people how far they had gone astray. Once the law became god, the law could no longer lead people to God. The law became the idolatry it condemned, there was no shortage of believers willing to worship their false god.

Anyone with a passing familiarity with the New Testament knows that Jesus and the Pharisees frequently squared off regarding the law, especially concerning the Sabbath. The law in its pristine form required that the Sabbath be kept holy. This was spelled out in minute detail. An observant Jew could walk only so far on the Sabbath, no cooking was allowed, no work was allowed. As far as we know, Jesus kept all of these strictures. But when it came to no healing on the Sabbath, Jesus set himself free. I doubt if the guardians of the law had a rule or an opinion about healing on the Sabbath. After all, how many people go around healing the blind, the lame, the deaf, and the mute? When Jesus healed, the authorities just automatically condemned him. Leadership is like that. When someone does something new or different, when someone does the unthinkable it must be wrong. The Church runs that way, General Motors runs that way, school systems run that way, as do our cities and towns.

There is no institution that is exempt from senseless laws. That should bother only those who expect the law to do their thinking for them. Jesus was not one of those people and neither should we be.

PRAYER ***O God, who gave us the commandment to love, help us remember that love cannot be contained in any law but can always be found in a grateful heart.***

THURSDAY OF THE THIRD WEEK

Yet they did not obey or incline their ear, but, in the stubbornness of their evil will, they walked in their own counsels, and looked backward rather than forward.

—JEREMIAH 7:23–28

The life of faith requires that we look both backward and forward if we are to keep our balance. Faith must be rooted in Scripture and tradition but lived in the here and now. This is not an easy task.

In my family home, now sadly sold but hopefully building happy memories for a new family, there was a corkboard on the kitchen wall, directly behind my father's chair and next to the doorjamb, that recorded the growth of my brothers and me. My mother was the keeper of the corkboard. When we were young, it was filled with box scores that mentioned our names and an occasional good report card (which were few and far between). As we grew and moved out, the board gathered post cards that chronicled our travels. At the top of the board was a bumper sticker that showed a team of dogs tethered to a sled and announced: "Unless you are the lead dog, the view never changes." Several years ago, when the auxiliary bishop in my diocese was given his own diocese, I shared with him the wisdom of the "lead dog" bumper sticker. Last year, when we sold my parents' home, I sent him the actual bumper sticker. He has a good sense of humor so he appreciated both the wisdom and the bumper sticker.

All of us need to be lead dogs when it comes to our faith. Instead of looking for new ways to live our faith, we fall back on what used to work and what used to challenge us. We do this long after the challenge has been absorbed into the fabric of our lives. The end result is a stale faith that is more comfort than challenge. I do not know who first said that the purpose of faith "is to comfort the challenged and to challenge the comfortable," but whoever said it was blessed with the wisdom of the Holy Spirit. It is a shame that too often we want the comfort of faith without its challenge.

PRAYER ***Help us, God, to be good stewards who can take from the storehouses of our lives things both old and new.***

FRIDAY OF THE THIRD WEEK

Jesus answered, "The first is, 'You shall love the Lord your God with all your heart, and with all your soul, and with all your mind and with all your strength.' The second is this, 'You shall love your neighbor as yourself.'"

—MARK 12:28–34

Love, love, love. Love God, love neighbor, love self. Most of us remember when the two great commandments seemed easy, but that was a long time ago, before the sins began piling up in our lives. Now we know that there are times when love is the most difficult of the virtues.

It is easy to love God when we have good health, a loving family, and a fulfilling job. It is difficult to love God when a child dies of cancer, we are betrayed by our beloved, and we are enduring a long period of unemployment. We thank God when we fall in love and curse God when that same love shrivels up and dies. We love good neighbors and avoid distasteful ones. We love the neighbor who shovels our walk and carries out our trash when we are no longer able. Quiet neighbors and neat neighbors are easy to love; noisy and sloppy neighbors are hard to love.

We love ourselves some of the time, but most of the time we are too hard on ourselves. We know all our faults and weaknesses. We are uncomfortably comfortable with our selfish choices. We eat too much, drink too much, and exercise too little, and that is not loving our bodies which are the temples of the Holy Spirit. When I was first ordained, there was a priest in the diocese who was short and very rotund. He used to pat his belly and say, "The body is the temple of the Holy Spirit but I have gone one step further. I am building a basilica and I have the dome all finished." It was funny the first time I heard it but sad every other time. He clearly did not love himself.

The Scriptures have it right—if we do not love ourselves we cannot love our neighbor and certainly cannot love God.

PRAYER ***Dear God, you are the greatest lover. Help us welcome your love so that our lives might be transformed.***

SATURDAY OF THE THIRD WEEK

Let us know, let us press on to know the Lord; his appearing is as sure as the dawn; he will come to us like the showers, like the spring rains that water the earth.

—HOSEA 6:1–6

Faith is all about knowing the Lord. Hosea the prophet makes it sound easy to know the Lord, and he is right. God makes it easy to know him, but we make it difficult! God is present to us in myriad ways. God's presence is as mysterious and as predictable as the sunrise and spring showers. We know the sun rises even when we cannot see it. We know that rain will come, but we cannot predict with any accuracy, even with all our sophisticated equipment, just when it will start or when it will end. Without the sun we cannot see; without the rain we cannot grow. Without God, we cannot see the truth and we cannot grow in virtue. We need to see God.

There is a touching story about a family that goes to church on Sunday. When they get home after Mass, the eleven-year-old daughter runs from the car and makes a beeline for her room, where she sits at her desk and begins to draw on a large piece of paper. Her mother is fascinated by her daughter's behavior. She watches her diligently from a distance for a while. Then the mother draws near to peer over her daughter's shoulder but cannot identify what she is drawing. She waits a few more minutes and then asks her daughter, "Honey, what are you drawing?" The daughter answers, "I'm drawing a picture of God." With maternal love and understanding the mother says, "But honey, nobody knows what God looks like." The daughter is unfazed and replies, "They will when I'm done."

That story puts a face on a familiar Scripture passage, "Unless you become like little children, you will not enter the kingdom of God." The world will never know God unless we show them what God looks like. The purpose of our lives, the challenge of our baptism, is to make our God known to the world.

PRAYER ***May we more fully believe that the purpose of our lives is to draw a picture of God that everyone can appreciate.***

FOURTH SUNDAY OF LENT

"My son," replied the father, "you are with me always and everything I have is yours. But we had to celebrate and rejoice! This brother of yours was dead and has come back to life. He was lost and now is found."

—LUKE 15:1–3, 11–32

In case you did not notice, this is the second time this Lent we have been treated to this gospel story. Why do we repeat the story of the Prodigal Son during Year C of the liturgical readings? Because the story has so much to teach us and has many levels of meaning.

God always rejoices when the lost are found. But the older brother in the story is unwilling to let his little brother back into his life. The younger brother sinned by not wanting any control over his life. The older brother sinned by having no concern for his wayward brother; he would not let himself feel his father's joy; he would not let his brother change. The younger son's sin was external; the older son's sin was internal. Both were sinners. Only one asks for forgiveness yet both were forgiven. The father goes out to greet the returning son while he is still a long way off; the father goes out to the older brother to invite him into the celebration. The father is the anxious agent of forgiveness for both sons. The parable reminds us that we need to greet returning sinners with warmth and understanding.

A young boy who had disobeyed his mother stormed out of the house when he was confronted with his disobedience. Some time later he returned home and was sneaking upstairs to his room. His mother saw him and asked where he was going. The boy said he was going to his room to talk to God. His mother asked if there was something he wanted to say to her before he talked to God. The boy said that if he spoke with her, she would just scold and punish him. He then delivered the line we should never forget and should always imitate, "God will listen to me. Then he will forgive me and forget all about it."

PRAYER

Help us, O God, to realize that every time we exclude someone from our lives, every time we will not let people change, we limit our experience of you.

MONDAY OF THE FOURTH WEEK

He went and begged Jesus to come down and heal his son, for he was at the point of death. Then Jesus said to him, "Unless you see signs and wonders you will not believe."

—JOHN 4:43–54

Jesus' miracles announced that he was the Messiah. Nevertheless, when the blind saw, the lame walked, and the sick were healed, those miracles became walls rather than windows to the Messiah. People then, like people now, wanted health more than faith. They wanted a God who would make them healthy, not a God who would redeem them; a God who would cure their physical rather than their spiritual ills.

Twelve-step groups never tire of preaching that we need to "let go and let God." Great advice. We need to accept that we are powerless in the face of our faults and failings, our sins. We need to cry out to our God that we are in need of salvation. We need to be more dedicated to God's will rather than our own. Too many of our prayers ask God to honor our will rather than vice versa.

Catherine Marshall wrote an article called, "When We Dare To Trust God," in which she tells the story of how she was cured of a lung infection that had her confined to bed for six months. The article tells how someone gave her a story about a missionary who contracted a strange disease which made it impossible to continue her missionary activity. The missionary prayed every day to be given the health to return to her missionary activity, but her prayers went unanswered. Finally one day, in total desperation the missionary cried out to God, "All right, I give up. If you want me to be an invalid, that's your business." Shortly thereafter the missionary got better. Ms. Marshall could not forget the story and finally was led to make her prayer in these words, "God, I am tired of asking for health. You decide if you want me sick or healthy." She too began to get better. Once we learn to trust in God there will be more windows than walls in our lives of faith.

PRAYER ***May the God of surprises help us to see windows where previously we have seen walls.***

TUESDAY OF THE FOURTH WEEK

Jesus said, "Do you want to be made well?" The sick man answered him, "Sir, I have no one to put me into the pool when the water is stirred up; and while I am making my way, someone else steps down ahead of me."

—JOHN 5:1–16

The sick man did not ask Jesus for help. Jesus asked him if he wanted help, which is rare indeed. Jesus does not intrude; he waits to be asked. Even here he asks, "Do you want to be made well?"

One of life's most difficult challenges is to ask for help. We all want to offer help. We even get upset when we find out that a friend was in need and did not ask for help. Unfortunately, the process is not reversible; our desire to be helpful is not often matched by our willingness to ask for help. I wonder why that is true.

Many years ago my mother taught me an important lesson. I was transferred from a parish where I had served for four years, and the parishioners wanted me to return for a thank you party. I was not interested in attending. They came up with several dates, and I was conveniently busy for each suggested date. Finally the contact person got exasperated with me and gave up. I thought I was out of the woods. Five minutes after the contact person hung up my phone rang again. It was my mother. She said in a tone that did not invite dialogue, "Joseph, you will be present on September 24th, you will be pleasant, and you will let them thank you." I protested but was shot down by these words, "You like to help people, you like to serve the needs of others. You will not deprive others from receiving joy by thanking you. I brought you up better than that!" Mom was right. I did attend and was glad I did.

Several years later I remember reading a Henri Nouwen book with this piercing comment, "If you can only give and not receive, the only honest thing to do is question why you give." Nouwen said it with polish; my mother said it with love. It is a message we all need to hear.

PRAYER ***Loving God, please help us let other people do for us what we are so willing to do for them.***

WEDNESDAY OF THE FOURTH WEEK

I can do nothing on my own. As I hear, I judge; and my judgment is just, because I seek to do not my own will but the will of him who sent me.
—JOHN 5:17–30

I have long since lost count of the number of people who have come to me wanting help in discerning God's will for them. I have also lost count of the times I have gone to others for help in trying to discern God's will for me. The truth be told, they and I already know what God wants us to do. What we are looking for is a loophole!

W.C. Fields was in the hospital near the end of his life. A friend went to visit and found Fields reading the Bible. The friend was taken aback because he knew Fields to be an atheist. The friend blurted out, "Why are you reading the Bible?" With complete honesty, Fields said, "I'm just looking for a few loopholes." An atheist looking for loopholes is one thing; believers looking for them is quite another.

More often than not God's will for us hurts. God's will pushes us deeper within ourselves and farther out of ourselves to meet the needs of others. God wants our selfishness to be transformed into selflessness, our apathy to become passionate concern, our anger to grow into forgiveness, our revenge to let go of the past and open us to the future. Into every place we have built a wall in our lives, God wants a door. God wants our undisciplined behavior to become disciplined, our distractions to become the seeds of contemplation.

There is no mystery about the will of God for us. God wants us to be motivated by loving care and concern for ourselves, our neighbors, and all of God's creation. Micah the prophet has told us all we need to know about the will of God: "He has told you, O mortal, what is good; and what does the Lord require of you but to do justice, and to love kindness, and to walk humbly with your God." All that remains is for us to act on God's will.

PRAYER ***Too often we mouth the words, "Your will be done." Help us to imitate Jesus who at the end of his life could say, "Not my will but your will be done."***

THURSDAY OF THE FOURTH WEEK

The Father who sent me has himself testified on my behalf. You have never heard this voice or seen his form, and you do not have his word abiding in you, because you do not believe him whom he has sent.

—JOHN 5:31–47

God always deals with us through intermediaries because we are not yet ready for the full, direct experience of God. We think we are but we are not. God knows us better than we know ourselves. God knows that our lives are filled with over-estimating our abilities. We perpetually think we are ready for the next step, but our parents, teachers, friends, and mentors know we are not.

It all starts very early in life. We think we are ready to stay up past our bedtime, but our parents know better. We are convinced that we are mature enough to take the car and stay out late into the night; once again parents know better. As young adults, we quickly become convinced that we are ready to marry the first time we fall deeply in love. Because wiser, more knowing individuals intervene, we grow to realize true love demands more than we are capable of giving so early in our adult lives. I was sure that I was ready to be a priest several years before the seminary faculty and the bishop decided to call me to priesthood. Thank God they prevailed. There is no telling how much harm I would have done in my early zeal. Life is all about growing into our premature evaluation of our capabilities. Those who love us hold us in check while nurturing and encouraging our continued growth. No easy task.

Jesus is the Word of God. We have not yet fully heard that word, so we are not yet ready for the Speaker of that Word. God is present in our family, neighbors, and friends, but too often we miss that presence. One day we will hear God's voice and see God's form, but only when we have grown enough to hear that Word and see that Form in everyday living.

PRAYER ***You have hidden your presence in our hearts. Only when we discover you in our hearts will we find you in our world. Help us discover your many hiding places.***

FRIDAY OF THE FOURTH WEEK

But after his brothers had gone to the festival, then he also went, not publicly but as it were in secret. The Jews were looking for him at the festival and saying, "Where is he?" And there was considerable complaining about him among the crowds.

—JOHN 7:1–2, 10, 25–30

Religion used to be a very public matter. We are far removed indeed from the days in Ephesus when disagreements about Christology led to cabbage-throwing in the marketplace. The magnificent cathedrals of Europe were built proudly by believers who wanted the world to know of their belief.

The parish where I presently serve is built on the fringes of our state university. Every year the incoming freshmen repeat a comical ritual. A student living in one the dormitories announces on Sunday evening that she is going out for a walk. She then leaves the dorm and sneaks up to church. Incoming freshmen are not comfortable saying, "I'm going up to Mass. Does anyone want to come with me?" Better to sneak out to Mass than be identified as a believer. Ironically, every stealthy believer eventually bumps into a fellow stealthy believer on the way to church. I doubt that anyone in the dormitory knows where they are going on Sunday evening but, at least, they get to walk together to the secret celebration of their faith.

We are all like that from time to time. We are closet believers living with the fear of being "outed." Our faith is private and personal. We do not want to impose our faith on others. Just the other day, I saw a member of the parish at a Monday daily Mass. She is not a regular at daily Mass. After Mass I asked if there were some special reason for her presence. She informed me sheepishly that she had had guests over the weekend and did not want them to feel uncomfortable by her going to Sunday Mass.

PRAYER ***Lord God, help us not to wear our religion on ourselves or hide it from view. Help us discover the witness value of a life lived in faith.***

SATURDAY OF THE FOURTH WEEK

Then the Pharisees replied, "Surely you have not been deceived too, have you? Has any one of the authorities or of the Pharisees believed in him? But this crowd, which does not know the law—they are accursed."

—JOHN 7:40–53

The Pharisees knew the law—that was fine. They hid behind that law—that was wrong. They thought the law would save them but the law did not then, nor does it now, have that power. Nevertheless, hiding behind the law is still popular. Martin Luther King, Jr., hit the nail on the head when he said, "They can make a law that says you cannot hate me, but they can never write a law that says you must love me."

Nothing is more sad than a believer hiding behind the law, and there is no shortage of laws behind which we can hide. Jesus left us with no laws, but he did leave us with a number of examples where the law did not fit the lived experience. The Pharisees were out to get Jesus because he broke the law. Jesus healed on the Sabbath. Jesus spoke with women in public. Jesus did not run away from sinners, but drew them near. Jesus was not some wide-eyed revolutionary, as some would have us believe. He knew and quoted the Scriptures freely. We are told on several occasions that he went to the synagogue on the Sabbath "as was his custom." The only reason Jesus was able to drive the money changers out of the temple was because he had gone to the temple to worship. We have every indication that Jesus was a good, observant Jew, but Jesus never hid behind the law. He observed the law but he knew there was something greater than the law—people in need. This is what separated him from the scribes and the Pharisees.

There is no better time than Lent to examine our consciences to see where we have become law-bound in our lives of faith. For our faith to be truly alive, we must root out all forms of legalism.

PRAYER ***In your wisdom, you have given us both the law and the prophets. May we never succumb to the temptation to find you only in the law.***

FIFTH SUNDAY OF LENT

The scribes and the Pharisees brought a woman who had been caught in adultery; and making her stand before all of them, they said to him, "Teacher, this woman was caught in the very act of committing adultery."

—JOHN 8:1–11

To fully appreciate the arrogance of the scribes and the Pharisees, we need to read a little of the seventh chapter of John's gospel. Jesus goes up to Jerusalem in secret for the Festival of Booths. He goes to the temple to teach, and the people flock to him because he "teaches with authority." On the last day of the festival he invites all who are thirsty to come to him. At this point, the scribes and Pharisees drag the woman caught in adultery before him. Jesus is teaching the people, the ones who are thirsty, and he is interrupted by their leaders who are not thirsty. They call him teacher but they will not let him be their teacher. All they want to do is discredit him so that they can control the people once again.

Is it any wonder that Jesus saves these words for the scribes and Pharisees, "Woe to you, scribes and Pharisees, hypocrites! For you are like whitewashed tombs, which on the outside look beautiful, but inside they are full of the bones of the dead and all kinds of filth" (Mt 23:27). Knowing how Jesus harbors special wrath for hypocrites should give all of us pause.

The scribes and Pharisees would have been better served if they worried about their own sins rather than the sin of the woman caught in adultery. We would be better served if we learned how to focus on our own sins rather than the sins of those around us. When Jesus says in today's gospel, "Let anyone among you who is without sin be the first to throw a stone at her," he is speaking not just to the scribes and Pharisees but to all of us.

PRAYER ***God of forgiveness, help us, the people who bear your name, to learn how to see the goodness in others and not dwell on their faults.***

MONDAY OF THE FIFTH WEEK

When they kept on questioning him, he straightened up and said to them, "Let anyone among you who is without sin be the first to throw a stone at her." And once again he bent down and wrote on the ground.

—JOHN 8:1–11

Why are we so intolerant of the sins of others? Why is it that we dwell on the failings of others while overlooking our own? This behavior has been around since Adam and Eve. Jesus called the people who do this hypocrites because they focus on the speck in their sister's eye while ignoring the plank in their own.

A pompous preacher mounts the pulpit one Sunday and rails away on the evils of lying. He bemoans the growing penchant for and acceptance of lying. He condemns the acceptance of so-called "white" lies. After a stirring half-hour sermon, he concludes with the dramatic flair for which he is famous. He pulls himself up to full stature and says to the congregation, "If God were to strike every liar dead, you know where I would be!" He lets the people come to their own conclusion, which has many of them smiling at the thought of the preacher being struck dead, and then he says, "I would be preaching to an empty church."

The congregation could only think of the preacher lying and the preacher could only think of their lying. No one focused on their own lying. The story works with the full range of sins. If God were to strike dead every thief, every adulterer, every curser, every drunk, every abuser, every racist, etcetera, etcetera, etcetera, where would we be? Without friends? No, we would be just as dead as they.

The message of today's gospel is, do not hang the past around the neck of others. Instead, offer them and ourselves the opportunity of the present and the future transformed by love. Jesus says to us over and over again, "Go and sin no more." We need to be better at saying this to the people around us.

PRAYER

Merciful God, help us to remember that we are not all sinners, we are all forgiven sinners.

TUESDAY OF THE FIFTH WEEK

So Jesus said, "When you have lifted up the Son of Man, then you will realize that I am he, and that I do nothing on my own, but I speak these things as the Father instructed me. And the one who sent me is with me; he has not left me alone, for I always do what is pleasing to him."

—JOHN 8:21–30

Jesus' confident faith came from the fact that he knew he was doing his Father's will. Our fickle faith flows from our selective response to God's will. Jesus knew he was sent by God; we are uncertain that God has chosen us and sent us to be his messengers. Our doubt flows from our thinking we are not worthy to carry God's message. We fear that our faults and failings will mute God's message.

The first thing we need to accept is that God chooses us freely: we do not earn God's choice. We do not have to earn God's love, indeed, we cannot earn it. We can waste a lot of time arguing with God about his selection process, or we can let ourselves be bathed in God's miraculous love. God knows us as we are—warts, pimples, blemishes, sins, faults, failings—the whole catastrophe, as a friend of mine is fond of saying. Nevertheless, he loves us and he calls us as we are. St. Paul had to struggle with his thorn in the flesh. We do not know what it was, but we know that Paul prayed for the thorn to be removed. God chose not to remove it, which led Paul to write these beautiful words: "Three times I appealed to the Lord about this, that it would leave me, but he said to me, 'My grace is sufficient for you, for power is made perfect in weakness.' So I will boast all the more gladly of my weaknesses, so that the power of Christ may dwell in me" (2 Cor 12:8–9).

Michelangelo, with his genius, was able to envision the magnificent statue of David in a piece of marble that others had rejected as flawed. God, with his love, is able to see the beauty in us when all we can see is our flaws. Perhaps the time has come to stop trying to tell God what he ought to see in us and begin to live what he does see!

PRAYER ***Lord, you have chosen us to be your messengers. Help us be confident that your strength will support our weakness.***

WEDNESDAY OF THE FIFTH WEEK

Nebuchadnezzar said, "Blessed be the God of Shadrach, Meshach, and Abednego, who has sent his angel and delivered his servants who trusted in him. They disobeyed the king's command and yielded up their bodies rather than serve and worship any god except their own God."

—DANIEL 3:14–20, 91–92, 95

I love this reading about Shadrach, Meshach, and Abednego in the fiery furnace because it is a wonderful example of trusting in God. I also love it because whenever I hear it, I am reminded of a time when I was a campus minister. There was one young coed who used to come to daily Mass on a fairly regular basis. From time to time I would ask her if she wanted to do a reading. She always said, "No," and I would always say, "Why not?" to which she would answer, "I might make a mistake." I ended this ritual exchange by saying, "Just trust in God and you won't make a mistake," which always brought a smile to her face.

As fate would have it, she came to Mass one day and, before I could ask her, she volunteered to read. The reading for that day was today's reading about Nebuchadnezzar, Shadrach, Meshach, and Abednego. I helped her practice the pronunciation of these difficult names, but she was leery. She trusted in God but about halfway through the reading she panicked, paused, and blurted out, "those three guys again." It was beautiful. She trusted, but she was also clever enough to be creative.

Today's reading invites us to examine where we let fear rule our lives. The Scriptures are full of the command, "Fear not." Nevertheless, too often we let fear determine how we live. How many poems have gone unwritten, how many paintings have gone unpainted, how many novels unpublished, how many speeches gone undelivered because the one inspired was afraid to share a talent? How many friendships never began, how many kind deeds never happened, how many times have the words "I love you" gone unspoken because the fear of rejection or of being misunderstood paralyzed the speaker or doer?

PRAYER ***May we have the insight to pray as if everything depends on God and work as if everything depends on us.***

THURSDAY OF THE FIFTH WEEK

Very truly, I tell you, whoever keeps my word will never see death.

—JOHN 8:51–59

It has been my privilege to see many people with deep faith embrace the death of loved ones or embrace their own death. Their faith will not let death win. Death hurts, death knocks them off their feet, they reel from death, but something deep inside them gives them the courage to embrace death and to know that life is stronger than death.

I have prayed with young and old as death approached. I have watched a peacefulness settle over their faces. I have seen their countenances shine as they say, "It is time," surrounded by family and friends who have said their last good-byes and professed their undying love. I have witnessed family ruptures heal in the face of death. My faith is strengthened by the peaceful acceptance of death, whether that acceptance is immediate or protracted. Those who keep God's word truly never see death.

The living dead are quite another story. Just who are the living dead? Those people whose selfishness has driven everyone out of their lives. The greedy whose possessions are more important than anything or anyone else. The angry who can see no good in the world. Those who are consumed with revenge. The hedonistic who are driven to search for the pleasure that will finally give meaning to their lives. Every time we let an argument fester, we are becoming the living dead. Every time we give begrudgingly, our living begins to die. Every time an unwanted pregnancy is aborted, the culture of death grows stronger. Every time a criminal is executed we wander farther and farther away from the word of God. Every time prejudice goes unchallenged, violence is unchecked, and lust runs rampant, our living is diminished.

The word of God tells us, "I have put before you life and death. Choose life that you might live." We need to understand that this word and our choices have far-reaching consequences.

PRAYER ***You, O God, are the giver of life. May we learn to see death as the door to fullness of life with you.***

FRIDAY OF THE FIFTH WEEK

If I am not doing the works of my Father, then do not believe me. But if I do them, even though you do not believe me, believe the works so that you may know and understand that the Father is in me and I am in the Father.

—JOHN 10:31–42

It is difficult to believe that a friend can lie to us, just as it is almost impossible to believe that an enemy is telling the truth. We listen to politicians with one set of ears, and we listen to friends with another set. In today's gospel the chosen people are too focused on Jesus and not on what he is doing. They have a preconceived notion of the Messiah and Jesus does not measure up. As a result, they are prevented from seeing that the blind see, the lame walk, and the poor have the good news preached to them.

We have the same problem. We all have a preconceived notion of how God is going to act and how God is going to enter our lives. Just before I received my present assignment, which has been a true blessing from God, I was rejected for another assignment. The priest who got the assignment had less experience than I had and was, in my opinion, less qualified for the job. When I was informed that I was not chosen for the job, I was first angry and then depressed. I felt that God had let me down. A month later, when I was named a pastor, all of the past hurt disappeared. I often wonder what would have happened if I had been chosen for the first assignment rather than the second.

That experience has taught me that what I want is often not what is best for me. What God wants always is. That is a very difficult lesson to learn. Several weeks after I was first named a pastor, my parents happened to meet the bishop. He said to them, "Is Joe happy?" Once informed that I was, he went on to say, "Good things always come to those who wait." My mother responded, "He knows that. Could the wait not be so long the next time?"

PRAYER ***May you bless us with patience as your will for us takes its final shape.***

SATURDAY OF THE FIFTH WEEK

The chief priests and the Pharisees said, "What are we to do? This man is performing many signs. If we let him go on like this, everyone will believe in him and the Romans will come and destroy both our holy place and our nation."

—JOHN 11:45–57

The chief priests and the Pharisees knew something had to change; they had the right question but the wrong answer. They were concerned about loss of power, loss of prestige in the community, and as a result they missed out on the opportunity to embrace the Messiah.

A priest came to me a few years ago. He was in a new assignment and he was confused. The people did not like him and their rejection was driving him further into himself. I asked him what he had done since arriving at his new assignment. After listening for a short while, I could see why the people did not like him very much. I told him I thought the people were correct in rejecting him. Believe me, that was not what he wanted to hear. He wanted me to tell him how to get the people to like him so he could exercise his power as pastor. I told him the people would like him when he made it clear that he cared about them. (He is still in that assignment and things seem to be going well, so I guess he changed his ways.)

Couples come to me with problems in their marriage. They ask, "What are we to do?" and are armed with a list of changes that their spouse should make. When I ask, "How can you change to improve your marriage?" they are at a loss. They have not thought about changing themselves; they have only thought of changing the other.

When we have problems with a boss, a friend, a neighbor, or a coworker, like the chief priests and Pharisees we tend to think that the solution lies in their changing their behavior. We cannot make decisions for others. We can only make decisions for ourselves. When we stop trying to change others and work on ourselves, our problems have a much better chance of disappearing.

PRAYER ***You have given us the gift of free will. We have the power of choice within us. Help us make better choices.***

PASSION SUNDAY

Hosanna! Blessed is the one who comes in the name of the Lord!

—MARK 11:1–10

Pilate, wanting to release Jesus, addressed them again; but they kept shouting, "Crucify, crucify him!" A third time he said to them, "Why, what evil has he done?"

—LUKE 23:1–49

For Palm Sunday to have its full impact, we need to reflect on two Scripture quotes. In the first account, the people shout out the praises of Jesus; in the second, the same people call for his death. In a few short days, the people go from praise to denial. It is a journey we have all made, from praise to denial and back to praise once again.

We go to church on Sunday. We sing all the songs. We serve the community as a lector or a minister of the Eucharist. We teach in the religious ed program. We bake for the parish bake sale. We volunteer for parish cleanup days. We join Habitat for Humanity and volunteer at the inner city soup kitchen. In doing so we give praise to our God. We shout, "Blessed is the one who comes in the name of the Lord!"

We also sin in a variety of ways. We cheat on our taxes. We file a false insurance claim. We steal from work. We are unfaithful to our vows. Prejudice rules our choices. We fail to control our tongues—we lie, gossip, curse, and insult others. In doing so we shout, "Crucify, crucify him!"

Palm Sunday offers the opportunity to learn from the very wise grandmother who took her unchurched granddaughter to a Pentecostal parish for Sunday worship. As the celebration built to a crescendo and all the worshippers were shouting "Alleluia!" and jumping up and down and praising the Lord, the granddaughter's eyes opened wide in amazement. Her grandmother leaned over and said to her, "It doesn't matter how high they jump. It is what they do once they land that really matters."

PRAYER ***God, our Savior, help us remember it is important that we give you praise, but it is more important that we do not continue your crucifixion by our sins.***

MONDAY OF HOLY WEEK

Mary took a pound of costly perfume made of pure nard, anointed Jesus' feet and wiped them with her hair. The house was filled with the fragrance of the perfume. But Judas Iscariot, one of his disciples said, "Why was this perfume not sold for three hundred denarii and the money given to the poor?"

—JOHN 12:1–11

True concern for the poor is powerful; bogus concern is transparent. Several years ago, the parish where I was stationed was trying to raise money to build a much-needed parish hall. During the fundraising stage of the project, I received a letter from a member of the parish who said that he was not going to give to the fundraiser because there were people starving all over the world. That letter really got under my skin. I wrote a rather blistering letter of response but never mailed it. (I highly recommend this practice!) What got to me was his glibness at telling me how we should allocate parish money. I would have been more inclined to listen to his suggestion if he had ever given any indication of being a generous contributor to any cause. If what he gave to his parish on a regular basis was any indication of what he was going to send to the starving of the world, then world hunger was here to stay.

The other side of the coin is represented by those who give and give generously to right the wrongs of the world. Recently a young member of the parish brought home to me the power of generous giving. This girl dropped a plain white envelope into the collection basket on the Sunday after she made her First Communion. Inside was some money and a note which said, "I want to share some of my First Communion money with a family in need." I need not mention that her family is very conscious of their commitment to share what they have with those who have less. This young girl had true concern for the poor because her parents showed her the way. I am confident that this concern will be a part of her life for many years to come.

PRAYER ***May we never stop looking for ways to share more generously the many gifts God has shared so generously with us.***

TUESDAY OF HOLY WEEK

After saying this Jesus was troubled in spirit and declared, "Very truly, I tell you, one of you will betray me." The disciples looked at one another, uncertain of whom he was speaking.

—JOHN 13:21–33, 36–38

The most amazing thing about today's gospel is that the disciples were uncertain about who would betray Jesus. Of course, all of them would, as all of us have! Our betrayals of our faith do not make us bad people, just incomplete Christians. In my own life, I struggle to live up to the words of faith that I too easily speak, and I know that I am not alone. We all have trouble living up to our faith commitment.

I do not know who said it, but I have taken great consolation in the saying, "The church is not a gathering of saints but a gathering of sinners who have not given up." We have all sinned and will sin again. We have all embraced the gift of faith and made wonderful choices, and we will continue to do so. As one sage put it, "There is a little bit of good in the worst of us and a little bit of bad in the best of us."

The challenge of being a good Christian is not to get puffed up by our virtues or deflated by our sins. If we can accept the sin in our lives, then we can accept sin in the lives of others. Once we accept sin, we do not have to spend so much energy hiding our failures. The energy we save can be used to root out sin from our lives. It was a very wise person who said, "When I was young, I used to wrestle with the devil and hope to win. Now I wrestle with God and hope to lose!"

Our sins consume too much of our attention and our virtues too little. It is a quirk of our nature to focus on the negative. Ten people can tell us we did a wonderful job; one person can criticize our performance. Unfortunately, too often we let the one voice drown out all the others.

PRAYER ***May our sins lead us to discover how dependent we truly are on God's loving forgiveness.***

WEDNESDAY OF HOLY WEEK

The Lord God has given me a well-trained tongue, that I might know how to speak to the weary a word that will rouse them.

—ISAIAH 50:4–9

We are all familiar with situations in which words failed us. A friend tells that her husband is leaving her and we struggle for the right words, but we settle for any words because we have to say something. Another friend tells us he has terminal cancer. We struggle for words. A coworker is fired, a child is killed, a roommate is raped, a son is arrested for drug possession, a neighbor's picture is plastered all over the front page of the morning paper because of a bribery charge. We search for words but they are hidden from us.

Recently, I was called to the hospital. A young couple were grieving an infant son dead at birth. I entered the hospital room filled with both sets of grandparents, the father standing by the bed. The mother was in bed cradling her dead child. I had my ritual prayerbook with me, but the prayers all seemed hollow. I was lost but my loss was dwarfed by the sadness that shrouded the room. I made the sign of the cross and read from the ritual. I began the prayer Hail Holy Queen, hearing for the first time the real meaning of "to you we cry, the children of Eve; to you we send up our sighs, mourning and weeping in this valley of tears." When that prayer was completed, I continued with the ritual, but the words on the page did not speak to the assembled family. And so I made up prayers as I went along. I assure you, the prayers were not my doing; they were a gift from the Holy Spirit. I trusted and God worked through me.

When confronted with a situation that leaves us at a loss for the right words, we can do no better than to imitate Isaiah and trust that our God will give us the words to rouse the weary, to comfort the lost and confused.

PRAYER ***May God help us grow ever more dependent on the gift of the Holy Spirit as we face the challenges of life.***

HOLY THURSDAY

For I received from the Lord what I also handed on to you, that the Lord Jesus on the night when he was betrayed took a loaf of bread, and when he had given thanks, he broke it and said, "This is my body that is for you. Do this in remembrance of me."

—1 CORINTHIANS 11:23–26

Jesus lived his life against the odds. His birth was not normal, his growing up unknown, his public life a mystery and a challenge. He was too laid back for his disciples and too forward for the leaders of Israel. He refused to be what others needed him to be. Instead, he gave himself over totally to doing the will of God, his Father, which is always a dangerous thing to do.

He spoke the truth to those who did not want to hear the truth. He sought out the disenfranchised. He treated the outcasts in a way that made them feel welcomed. The blind, lame, deaf, and deformed found in him a friend. He told his disciples and all who would listen that the only thing that mattered was to live a life of love. When he knew that those who opposed him were ready to silence him by death, he did not lash out. Instead, he gave his disciples one final image of how to love. He gathered with them to celebrate the Passover meal, a meal which spoke to all of them of their history as a chosen people who had been oppressed, a meal that reminded them of how God had saved them from slavery, how God had led them to freedom by the blood of a lamb.

Jesus blessed bread and shared; he blessed wine and shared. He told them that in the blessing and sharing they would always have the best reminder of the love of God. Bread and wine, simple gifts shared at a table, made special because they were broken and shared in love. No meal, no celebration will ever be the same. Every piece of bread served and each glass raised in a toast now speaks of God.

PRAYER ***Loving God, by your love you have transformed our lives. May we never break bread without giving thanks to you for being present to us at every table. May we always be reminded of you when food is transformed by love into a meal.***

GOOD FRIDAY

When Jesus knew that all was now finished, he said, "I am thirsty." So they put a sponge filled with sour wine on a branch of hyssop and held it to his mouth. When Jesus had received the wine, he said, "It is finished." Then he bowed his head and gave up his spirit.

—JOHN 18:1—19:42

The message of his cross, the message of every cross is that there is strength in weakness. There is no shame in being needy. There is no shame in crying out for help. Yet Jesus' final lesson is the most difficult to follow. We hate to be needy; we hate to ask for help. When I look at the relatively few crosses that have been part of my life or when I reflect on the crosses that others have been asked to carry, one thing is certain: those crosses were never carried alone. We all need and have been blessed with a Simon of Cyrene, who helps carry the crosses that enter our lives.

Jesus cried out, "I am thirsty." When life turns dark, we need to follow the example of Jesus and ask for help. When the cross enters our lives, we should reach out for help. Jesus got sour wine, but it was enough. The help we get might be very ordinary. A friend may sit with us and listen to our troubles. A teacher might give us a little extra help. A priest may raise his hand to extend absolution. A sister might cry with us or help us laugh in the face of adversity. A neighbor might bring over a casserole or a sinfully rich dessert. A brother might sit on the back steps and share a beer. All we have to do is say we are in need.

Our crosses have the power to weigh us down, to crush us, but they can also be invitations to ask for help. A shared cross is always lighter. Jesus helped all who came to him in need, but before he could say, "It is finished," he needed to open up and ask his executioners for help. Our lives will never be finished or fulfilled until we learn to receive help as freely as we give it.

PRAYER ***Jesus, Son of the living God, help us follow your example and ask for help when the cross or the shadow of the cross enters our lives.***

EASTER VIGIL

The women were terrified and bowed their faces to the ground, but the men said to them, "Why do you look for the living among the dead? He is not here, but has risen."

—LUKE 24:1–12

It is easy to look for the living among the dead. We are so used to old answers that we no longer hear new questions. We settle for less without being aware. We look for God in old prayers and find an old God. We look at people we love with tired eyes and fail to see the newness in them. We trudge through another workday, and where once our motivation was to make a difference, now we are satisfied to make it through the day. Life has lost its meaning and we are bored.

Easter is all about newness. Our biggest challenge is to discover newness in the familiar. The women in today's gospel went to visit the grave of a friend and teacher and were confronted with an empty tomb. Nevertheless, they return to the apostles and tell them what they have seen. Peter races to the tomb and sees the emptiness and the linen cloths. He, like the women before him, goes home amazed at what he has seen. In truth, they were amazed at what they had not seen. They expected a grave but found a door—an open door that invited them to newness. In faith they walked through that door, and life was changed.

If we have made our lenten journey in faith, today should present us with an open door, a door to the future, a door to newness. May we all have the trust to make the leap of faith that is Easter's greatest gift.

PRAYER ***Alleluia, Christ is risen! He is risen indeed! Thank you, Jesus, for making this lenten journey with us.***

TWENTY-THIRD PUBLICATIONS
BAYARD PO BOX 180 • MYSTIC, CT 06355
1-800-321-0411 • FAX: 1-800-572-0788 • E-MAIL: ttpubs@aol.com

9 781585 951284